Creation

A poem of eternal love and infinite space

by

Stephen Livesey Ashworth

Cover design by Espthen Thorwash

To: Liz (wherever you may be)

and Neil and Buzz
and the millions who gave them their place in history

and Aleksandr Sergeyevich P.

*

I would build that dome in air . . .
— Samuel Taylor Coleridge

*

Copyright © Stephen Livesey Ashworth 1999
Published by Astronist Publishing, Oxford, UK
Tel. Oxford (01865) 250290
E-mail sa@astronist.demon.co.uk

All rights reserved
ISBN 0-9536158-0-4
Set in 10-point Bookman on the Macintosh
Printed by Kall Kwik, Oxford

Creation

Upon the living brink of crystal deeps
Stood the Designer with sky-challenging gaze.
A crumb of bread – he mused – a sip of wine
Vanish among ten billion trillion suns
That chime slow eons of galactic time.
What hope that ever mortal flesh and dreams
Could overcome these stark infinities?

The full moon sparkle-paved the midnight bay
Where whispering couples jay-walked hand in hand:
Stone death illuminated lustful play.
With fumbling eyes and lips they sought to raise
Their nature's business to another stage.
Begotten of the senseless dirt, their love
Would animate the Earth. – But, above,

Through silent spaces roasted by the sun,
Chilled by the night and starved of oxygen,
It turned: a Passchendaele of violence past,
Of tumbled highlands, blasted lava plains,
The pale gravestone to a still-born world.
Up here no busy glob of primal clay
Had woven costly daisy chains of DNA.

No tree had offered shade; no bird had flown;
No flower ever woke to greet the dawn;
No river ever flowed; no breeze was blown
Across the slag; no song was ever heard;
No rampant stag; no birth; no death; no angry storm
Of passion; and no reconciliation –
Just ashen rocks and cosmic radiation.

Then something happened. Out of the primordial void
A chariot of fire spread its landing struts
To settle gently on the virgin dust.
When Neil and Buzz took breaths of bottled air,
Their gift of tongues baptised the deaf-mute stones
With speech: *The Eagle's landed – How magnificent*
The desolation all around the LM!

Not everybody cheered. Is it not sick –
They sneered – to fire off into heaven's vault
This daredevil circus trick of astronauts,
While millions starve and millions suffer pain
And wars around the globe drive us insane?
Best spend our money binding up our wounds –
Hah! It's no concern of ours what's on the Moon!

And yet – he thought – can *men that strove with gods*
Fail to exult with such technologies?
Now Zarathustra offers us this chance
To wade the shallows of the cosmic seas,
To teach the dismal dust to breathe, to plant
A lunar Garden of Tranquility,
And raise a lunar Adam, lunar Eve!

Oh, let me live and not exist in vain!
I want to build the Tower of Babel to the sky,
And brave the crash, survive and build again.
Oh, let me love and love too deeply you,
Who twist my dreams around your precious name,
And let us quarrel, hate – then weeping through
Our sorrow seek repentance, love anew!

*   *   *

A hundred years have passed, and on the Moon
The seed men's rockets impregnated comes to bloom.
Where once the frozen rockscape lay unchanged,
Dormant as any fossil, where dour shades
Of grey painted a savage slumbering face,
A joyful flame of colour leaps and twists,
And forges in the desert a metropolis.

I love you, city of another world!
Child of old Earth, yet with a joie de vivre
Filled: your rabbit warrens underground;
Your golden domes that dazzle in the sun;
Your liquid opal shield of artificial skies
Embracing *many an incense-bearing tree* –
Machine and ecosphere in harmony.

I love your spaceport, where the people throng.
Where once a meteor strike disturbed the long-
Quiescent vastness once per million years
Now tourists, academics, politicians,
Models, artists, singers, engineers,
Shake hands, embrace and kiss in the café –
Arrivals and departures every day!

Gaze at these ramparts holding the vacuum out,
The life-force in, the vital readings tight;
Gaze, Earthling visitor, and be amazed
To see a skin of diamond fibre spun
By countless nano-spiders; see these bones
Of basalt honeycomb, these nerves of light;
These leaves of silicon unfreeze the nerveless night.

And high above the domes, where people fly
On nylon wings of high-tech magic joy,
Far, far above the UN Conference Centre,
Striking dumb the loudest faction-leader,
Hovers the blue-white globe in splendrous grace,
The island home in space, perpetual muse,
Proud mother – profitable market place.

Contain your envy, Earthling, if you can,
Of those who found a lunar destiny –
This happy breed of men, this little world,
This precious gem set in the velvet sea,
This engineering triumphs' brightest pearl.
Why grumble that it's only for the wealthy few?
The troubled poor can celebrate the inspiration too.

And even the Designer stands in awe
Of what his students brought forth in his name:
Immortal city! Oh, undying fame!
He did not wish to miss more than he must:
Although his bones have crumbled into dust,
A thought brings all desires within his grasp –
They wired his living brain up in a bubbling flask.

Shine on, you hopeful beacon to the world,
And demonstrate how peace and reason flower:
Your branches are the sky, your roots on Earth,
Your craters are transformed to rings of power.
Titanic city, you are practically
Indestructible by Nature's wrath –
Your strength inspires the technocratic myth!

>But – Far beyond human ken,
>Unseen by living sense,
>Orbiting restlessly,
>Shifting uneasily,
>Hovers the berg with a burden of ice,
>Loose planetesimal drifting in space
>All these years.

>Nemesis is my name,
>Chaos is where I roam,
>Ringing past Saturn, I
>Sling off again alone,
>Skirting Uranus, unstable my course,
>Balanced on tightropes of gravity force
>Through the stars.

* * *

Amid the precincts of Tranquility
The hubbub of the business day draws to a close.
Ten thousand lunar boomers flood the streets:
First dinner, then to the award-winning shows!
Stocks are up and interest rates are down
As banks on Earth revalue lunar coin.
The word from the President is sterling joy.

Two killed while working in Copernicus
On new construction; safety rules will all
Be redesigned. A well-known senator –
Caught in a call-girl's knickers; now they call
Resign! Resign! That notorious centre-forward
Reveals his transfer for a crazy sum.
The Space Girls' latest hit's at number one.

And as the domes and boulevards begin
To fool the eye with make-believe evening gloom,
A junior technician weaves commands
Into an electronic tapestry;
He switches off the screen; he stretches, stands,
Relaxes with a mug of ersatz tea.
His eyes are brimming bright with sharp expectancy.

And while the city raves its stress away,
And jazzy beats vibrate its diamond streets,
Eugene ardently bullies the time,
And paces up and down his small domain,
Watches the news and has a bite to eat –
But every moment scans, antenna-thought,
The street outside, the passage leading to his door!

A newsflash: and astronomers have spotted
Diving towards us a formerly unknown comet.
There should be a spectacular display –
A vasty scimitar unsheathed in space
As if in ghastly warning – but the experts claim
There's no cause for alarm. The comet's path
Will do no harm to those on Earth or Moon.

Scheherazade, come and dance with me!
Bring me your radiant sable face, your velvet hair,
Your two-tone hands, your caring touch, your grace,
Your laughing lighthouse-eyes that beckon me,
This wrecked survivor drifting on the sea,
To chase the eternal harbour of your light –
Let's trace again the rendezvous we danced last night!

A footstep in the corridor, a ring,
And Eugene's heart bursts into song. Trembling
In every finger he flings wide the door.
It is . . . not her. He greets his best friend, Alec,
Who in earnest speech laconic and prophetic
Confides: Too long man dreamt he was the master –
This new comet is an omen of bad karma.

Eugene smiles, but listens distantly.
His inner eye distils a gentler face,
His calendar is marked with happier dates
And grander memoranda of good times to be.
Champagne and ice-cream just for two – he muses –
A mountain hike, a voyage in the Med,
Paris in springtime, and a king-sized four-post bed!

And soon we two will learn to dream as one.
Returning to the Moon, we'll weave and weld
Our shared household, and I'll be so thrilled
When you enfold me in your fashion world.
And when at last we match and purl our genes,
Conceive ourselves a baby boy or girl,
Who knows what scenes of joy that might unfurl!

You enshrine in your elegant physique
A holy icon of African and Arabic.
My own genetic line is, truth to tell,
Accounted as a failed experiment.
Conceived in vitro from the Designer's cell,
I missed my theoretical development –
But I'm still the designer clone of one so eminent!

Thus Eugene sketches out his future bliss:
Ten thousand and one Arabian nights he'll sail away
Together with his clever chocolate princess.
With her to sing new fire into his soul
He'll scale the wheels of the lunar high-tech biz
And seize his place, chase a salary
That matches his star-quality heredity.

*   *   *

A week spins past, a month Earth-phases by.
The comet extends its ghostly emanation
And chilly haunts the morning sky. It flies
Closer to the solar conflagration,
And as it dives past speedy perihelion
The heat infuriates its sleepy volatiles,
Which now erupt in rage for millions of miles.

Emergency! Alarm! The fatal berg,
Observing Newton's laws, especially the third,
Has turned its course. Computers hum and spin
Cobwebs of numbers, scrambling to ensnare
Its new intent – aaah?! – unlikely though it be,
The intruder in the firmament has precisely
Targeted . . . the City of Tranquility!

On every channel President Smith appeals for calm.
His family and he, he says, will scorn
Approaching danger, and remain at their
Official home in Armstrong pressure dome.
Now the Designer, from his glass decanter,
Lets it be known he has matured a plan
To save the city from the grim marauder.

But the smart money's already bailing out of the gilded gates;
Tickets to Earth sell for a hairy sum:
Alec grits his teeth and pays the premium.
To Eugene he confides he does not rue
His life upon the Moon, but now the time has come:
He's made a tidy pile, and so – goodbye,
Man never was meant to live up in the sky!

Eugene sighs, distracted, listlessly –
Too true: the higher you fly, the harder you fall.
Alec stares with friendly scrutiny,
Perceives the acid gall of private sorrow
Etching Eugene's cheeks, the groans of sleepless weeks –
What's up, old fellow? A family death? A bust-up
With your girl? Too bad. Oh well, I must rush.

And Alec flies. It's time to catch his rocket.
He checks a seventh time his bag, his passport
And his ticket out of the City of Dreams
That dreamt one dream too far. Away, away!
Back to Mother Earth before the break of day
When dreams that once inspired implode to nothing.
Alec grabs his seat, feels the engines gushing.

And Eugene . . . rows his solitary boat
Across the Lake of Tears towards a shore:
He scales the mist-hung cliffs of the Isle of Hope,
Groping in his blindness for a cause,
A reason to explain the cruel joke.
Now blazing words engage his emptiness;
They char the page with bewildered tenderness –

Dear Scheherazade, treacle love,
Do you remember how we gazed at Earth
Together, wished upon a star above?
They say you've moved to another flat.
I tried your e-mail but I can't connect.
Scheherazade, darling, please reply –
Did I not whisper in your ear our love must never die?

He posts the letter to her college box,
And marvels at the quiet of the streets:
The halls of money-making now recall the smell
Of hushed foreboding. – Er, excuse me, why are
These trains not running? Why these galleries locked?
Look around: these shops have all closed down!
Where is everybody in this town?

Some sparked the electric path to Copernicus,
Or sanctuary seek in Tsiolkovsky.
Hundreds throng the orbiting space terminus,
Earth-shuttle booked. Those brave souls left behind
Now sweat with friends and dread the approaching time.
The President? Well, everyone's long known:
His virtual self is with us; the real one's flown!

Eugene, pondering, turns away, alone.
His wandering leads him to a long parade:
A tree-columned nave under a mosaic dome.
The cedars reach towards the stained-glass canopy
That hovers in suspended symmetry –
But is these ancient wizards' incantation
For heavenly blessings, or violent immolation?

Five trillion tons of surplus Genesis ice,
Express despatch: that'll set a few Martinis shaking! . . .
But, my darling, did you reach
A refuge from the threatened reckoning?
If only you would tell. Oh, how it aches
To think you still could be so near to me!
I'd hold your hands and kiss your face so tearfully:

Did I say something sour? Did I offend
In the hour of love? So long ago it seems!
Was I too sharp, did I come on too strong,
Pursuing mine, forgetting you too have dreams?
Your muslin-hidden eyes remain inscrutable,
And now I fear the sky's about to fall:
My darling, break your silence, please call!

In desperate need his eyelids close in prayer;
His mind-stretch to a telepathic touch
Rebuilds her essence from the slippy air –
The thought of you electrifies my sight!
What spiteful Fate, what comet strike can break our circuit
When my charge of love to you returns? . . .
The cedars gaze down on him unconcerned.

A plaintive cry draws Eugene's eye around:
Between the buildings, distant half a mile,
There hovers the silhouette of a child,
Lost, perhaps, abandoned in the panic.
Eugene hurries in slow-motion bounds
To help, but the child has vanished without a trace . . .
A dog barks far away . . . a breeze chills Eugene's face . . .

And all this while, the juggernaut express
Tears silently the space-time tapestry
Along the single thread from west to east
That leads to lunar crash convergency.
The people skyward stare in rare expectancy:
All still looks normal, while the stars rotate,
Mock-innocent of the fate long since predestinate.

The Designer has no truck with cowardice
Engarbed with haute-couturish resignation,
Or guarded quasi-religious humbleness.
His city was not built on superstition,
So neither shall he pray for its salvation.
Numbers scroll, virtual worlds unfold and gyre;
He inputs now the timely order: Fire!

And on a battlesat a million miles in space
A fusion surge discharges an energy deluge
Into the largest laser of the age.
And as his students cheer and whoop their joy,
The icy outer soil shrieks and boils:
A streak of spoil erupts from a craterous crack,
And wrenches the lumbering comet onto a different track.

Oh halleluya! Sing the Designer's praise!
Let pop opinion on Earth and Moon
Dazzle the ether with acclaim; let Hollywood
Commemorate his fame, and merchandise!
The human tide reverses: joyfully
The refugees turn homeward, breathe a sigh. –
The comet smiles benignly in the evening sky.

Our lovelorn hero haunts the arrival lounge
In forlorn hope that chance will reunite
Him with his pretty, laughing ebonite.
His gaunt eyes scorn the silken sheets of porn,
His forehead furrows at the sight of warm
Embraces, handshakes, kisses in the café,
As those who fled now come home to stay.

Again he fumbles out his true love's number:
Access denied. He posts another query
Through the virtual face of the database, input
With a reverent kiss. Deep down he knows it's hopeless.
Now he sees Tranquility revive with vitality
He cannot share. Alone, he tries to disperse
Despair by rafting out some lines of verse.

And while he floats combining rhyming sounds,
Scheherazade puts on earthly weight,
Stares from her Skylon seat at the approaching ground.
A troubling thought clouds her Abyssinian brow;
Now and then she hooks her hair back
Over her ears, reaches for the phone,
Whispers his name, hesitates . . . then puts it down.

And thus the sanguine hue of resolution
Is sicklied over with self-conscious doubt,
And letters that should be wrote, phone calls made,
Remain unknown and private, notional, contemplate.
She purses her magnuscious full-lipped mouth:
I'm sorry, Gene, but this is how it had to be;
I hope you understand, you're not too mad at my timidity.

The planet slips towards her, misty wisps
Flash past the stubby wings. The tarmac rushes up.
The Skylon touches, runs. The seats vibrate.
Pale sunshine on her face. She waits her turn to alight,
Tunes her headphones to the Firebird Suite.
Eugene's vain delight now makes her womb dilate –
You've got me in the club, you reprobate!

*   *   *

And so the steaming, fire-scarred cosmic guest,
Like a streaming firework frozen in mid-burst,
Watches over the deep both night and day.
Closer it advances, till its tail
Binds the heavens in an arch of frost.
With uncompromising haste through the portal we must pass –
That breathes on the Moon with an alien stardust kiss.

Eugene has resumed his drab employment,
Embroiders code for lunar industry,
Relaxes with a mug of ersatz tea,
Without recovering such glad enjoyment.
His eyes are sadder now, yet he sees
An answer to his prayer. His hour of need
Has taught him how to dare emergency:

When life lies bleeding in the dust so desolate,
And when you stagger with a stake-pierced heart
Through graveyards, cold, alone, disconsolate,
And hope flings up a noose around your throat
And mocks you with its grandiose futility
And chokes you with your raging inability
To understand: Why is this happening to me? –

There comes at last a hallowed spot of calm,
A shaft of moonlight draws you from your unquiet tomb.
This is my reality . . . yet, this is my dream:
These opposites contain a steady gaze
That faces the abyss with equanimity,
Accepts the turmoil, agony and nightmare,
Nods, and simply says: Yes, I was there.

The dice against us? Outlook trouble-filled?
Well set your purpose, end your plaintive grousing,
Be a Beowulf or a fair Brunnhilde,
A Wallace Hartley or an Ida Straus!
For each of us must say in our own way:
My God, oh why hast thou forsaken me?
Why hast thou sunk my confident technology?

And thus inspired, Eugene sails through
The luminescent causeways of the city,
Like a man who, dreaming, fears to wake
And lose a vision of such exoticity.
Strangers flash by, snail-horn-eyed, so strange:
They fail to greet him, follow their own noses,
Do not recognise their mutual symbiosis.

Now Eugene strides the Halls of Destiny,
Bathes in the liquid voices rippling
Off hanging balconies, heroic friezes –
A cog . . . but still a cog of joy and grief,
Enmeshed within an internet of souls,
Friends, all – yet, missing his houri's face,
Tranquility remains an empty echo space.

*   *   *

A square, a fountain, and a melody
Of iridescent sculpture on the costly grass –
And here a man falls groaning painfully;
He wrestles with a phantom in a bed of flowers,
Does not have the power to get up.
Bystanders stop and ask what's wrong and strive
To reassure him: help will soon arrive.

Above their heads, a champagne-spray of light
Celebrates President Smith's descent in triumph:
The plan to use a laser satellite
Was his, his was the finance and the science!
The Designer played a minor role. So vote
For five more years of Smith on election day! –
Two paramedics carry the sick man away.

And now the silvery rainbow in the stars,
Its prophecy done, fades into the black.
The tail that seeded lunar crater fields
Grows small and flaccid, drowsy, wilted, slack.
In Aldrin dome the Grand Theatre opens,
To surf the zeitgeist with a comic smash-hit yarn
Of love and cold betrayal and a comet-crash alarm.

On opening night the poor romantic lead
Goes down with a mysterious disease.
What a shocker in this day and age,
When electronic doctors gauge us inside out,
Forestalling coughs and colds and cancer sprouts
And all such bugs and aches and pains that tire us –
Until a bearded microscoper stammers: V- V- Virus!

A billionaire collapses in his bath;
A lady tour-guide stumbles to her knees
And retches on her humble lunch in front of twenty
Startled stares. A child dreams of death.
The President is missing half his staff.
The tiny hospital is overwhelmed
With vital signs threbbing to a painful end.

A new infection cheats the antiseptic ring
Of medical protection. But – where from?
Have we caught something from the comet's heavy breathing?
Or has it wakened ancient demons? Or the domes
Harboured eco-disaster all this time? Who knows?
Enmired in microbial anxiety,
Tranquility is not such a tranquil place to be!

Officials in the stylish spaceport lounge

Gaze in amazement at the ugly scrummage

When laughing new arrivals, homeward-bound,

Are countered by a sudden outward rush

Of haggard faces, clutching bag and baggage.

Tempers flare; policemen fast appear –

Halt! Only ticket-holders pass through here!

The epidemic spreads like scandalous news.

Now long-forgotten ghosts and ghouls emerge,

Spreading sickness and insanity

And antique dread of mass calamity.

The dead lie dying in the lavish avenues.

Long thought banished to a superstitious age,

A cruel Jehovah strikes them down in vengeful rage.

Numb terror fills the wide eyes of a child

Whose mother's desperate Why?! remains ignored.

Grim rumours circulate of secret tests

With bio-warfare agents; or of fatal flaws

Long covered up; or that the President

Has crashed trying to flee the City of Death;

That Earth has quarantined the lunar pest.

Whole families in space-suits make a run
Across the skyless, breathless waste outside.
They only have twelve hours oxygen
To last a marathon of two hundred miles.
All mobiles, gone; all rockets, long since launched,
And gate-crashed smaller settlements' capacity
With refugees from the plague-struck city.

Eugene stays at home and locks the door.
He stuffs his pillows in the ventilation.
While counting chocolate biscuits in the cupboard store
He estimates the chance of suffocation.
Now he hacks into the security net:
Through television and his IT skill,
Eugene virtually roams the streets of the city at will.

On every corner, crouched pathetically,
Or scurrying past, pale-faced beneath a mask –
Quick, switch to close-up! Could that person be – ?
Eugene tenses, ready to plunge out
And save his loved one in his lifeboat-home,
But no such luck. Of course, she's long since gone,
And left me with my sinking memories alone.

Now Eugene switches to a leafy view
With statues of philosophers and engineers.
Where once impulsive joyful crowds thronged through
The famous Boulevard of the Pioneers,
A pair of looters shimmy past the good and the great;
They haul their useless booty down the street,
And trample on the dying with defiant feet.

Yet all is not despair. Standing tall
In Parliament Square a man surveys the panic.
In evening dress, a face one half-recalls,
He calmly sips a bulbous glass of cognac
And waits his turn for death with quiet unconcern.
His blue cigar smoke says: I've lived my best.
A top-range robo-Jeeves buttles at his behest.

A soap-box Jeremiah gloats: And thus the Holy Will
Uncloaks all worldly beauty to reveal
A grinning mask of lies! Eugene cries,
Weeping for the lovely face of one he knew:
A girl whose aspect promised much. And now
An ill-starred city on the cusp. Suddenly
The watcher senses he is being watched.

Submerging in the underworld of colour-shimmer,
He sees a man who, like him, is enrobed
In a shining garment of computer code.
His face is Eugene's own, as in a mirror
That reflects advancing years. His eyes are proud,
As if his city must withstand all wrongs unscathed –
But does the idol stand on feet of bronze?

Eugene's tearshot vision floods with crimson glaze:
How could you dare a mission of such folly?
To teach the dismal dust to breathe, to raise
A city where no city ought to be?
Your greed created this monstrosity,
Where innocents now cough up their lives to satisfy
Your craving for construction in the sky!

And why did you engender me, unasked?
My life is wrecked. My failure is unmasked
Because I cannot give the love that girls expect.
I am the product of your twisted genes,
I'm helpless to control my destiny,
And soon I'll join the dreaming throng of death:
My life – mere comet dust, my passion – what a
   waste of breath!

Don't make me weep! – the Designer shrieks in answer –
Was it for nothing that, despite my cancer
Ward, my failing sight, my faithless wife,
I drew the Moon into the sphere of life
And raised a lunar Adam, lunar Eve?
But now my city bleeds. You muddle-brains,
Why don't you buckle down to work and heal its pains!

And work is all that's left. Now Eugene picks
The trail up from sickly ailing hands,
And passwords into the medical software banks.
Virtual servants rise at his command,
A green-skinned Kermit and a Gandalf grey,
And with their aid and his designer luck,
At last – his program isolates the pesky bug!

The antidote is bottled, but – too late . . .
Too late for any lunar soul's salvation.
The Designer's weary cerebrum sparks its last;
Eugene slumps onto the floor with enervation.
A call from Earth! – but he is too far gone to answer.
His dull eyes close the book on mortal ardour,
The last word on his leaden lips . . . Scheherazade!

* * *

The Space Age stalls. Hedonistic cynics
Press the joystick down a voluptuous dive.
The spotlight picks out wars and social antics,
Buy-outs, sell-offs, cock-ups, terror strikes.
Frail footholds on the lunar lava plains
Or perched upon a martian canyon rim
Gamble death against survival: times are grim.

Until . . . a footfall echoes on the tiled floor,
Disturbs the dust of forty years in Aldrin dome:
A woman gazes round in reverent awe
To penetrate the sanctum, see the vaulting span,
The lavish high relief, the spiral columns,
The legendary pile thousands once called home . . .
The air is rotten with decaying bones.

Where once cascading cliffs of strings and brass
Brought to life The Isle of the Dead,
Where once the Sleeping Beauty and Prince Charming danced,
Today an eerie stillness holds its breath . . .
The dreaming domes, the silent subway labyrinths,
Await their prince to reawaken with a kiss
The eternal life/death/re-birth calculus.

She turns. Transglucent spacesuits gleam. She speaks.
The troops applaud Commander Firebird.
She combines in her elegant physique
Dusky Afro-Arabic with the Designer's word
Transmitted through a junior technician
Of whose life and love not many have heard.
She's stubborn as her mother, and an academician.

She distributes a thousand patient jobs:
The city's air is filtered, soil is checked,
Trees, plants, fishes rescued from neglect
By boozing, swearing decontamination squads.
White-coats delve into the science archives,
Discover there the secret of the virus
Worked out long ago by some unknown genius.

But can you guarantee to sterilise
The city, safe for humans to return? –
Enquires a talking head with cool surprise:
Exposer of corruption, mis-spent funds,
Hypocrisy and hubris, greed and lies.
Firebird's smile now graces a million videos:
The pressure's on her to announce good news.

No problem! – she reports, with dancing eyes –
The parks, the shops and offices are cleansed,
Inhale the freshest air that money buys!
The bio-hazard's tale is at an end,
Our presbyopic sponsors watch their profits rise. –
A stretcher with a squaddie doubled in pain?
She deftly steers the cameraman the other way.

An urgent call draws Firebird aside.
She leaves the gabble of media folk behind,
Crosses a cloistered courtyard broad and wide,
Then down a marble staircase she descends,
Bounding like a puma down the mountainside.
Echoes of reverent music from candle-lit rooms
Accompany Firebird into the makeshift catacombs.

This way! – The Superintendent guides her past
Dumb black-bagged rows of numbered tragedy.
He unzips one, allowing her to see. –
We found this photo of your mother by his heart.
We thought you'd like to know. – She stares aghast:
Long time she dare not kiss the vacant skull
Until her trembling hands, her smarting eyes are still.

Awake, you domes! Rise up, you streets, and walk! Revive!

These dead we lay to rest beneath the perfumed trees.

In the arrival lounge, new voices strive

To banish past disaster with buoyant harmonies.

A younger generation breathes ambition,

And sketches even grander city plans

To embellish lunar maria and the martian sands.

New spacecraft prod the tumbled craterscape,

New roots of steel turn the stubborn soil.

Through years of toil, one voice rings out above them all –

See how the panoply of life is one!

See how all nations share the same place in the sun!

We draw our inspiration from the day

When men first set their bootprint in Tranquility.

Shine on, you fertile midwife to the cosmos,

And demonstrate how love and courage flower:

Your children are the stars, your mother, Earth,

Your craters, wedding cups of sacred power.

Olympic city, you are built upon

The suffering of those who went before –

Your triumph is the tribute to their woe!

A thousand years flow by: the double world
Now comes of age, the Moon has life enough.
The first millennial project is fulfilled:
Blue skies below reflect blue skies above.
They say that life began on one of these,
But which one? The smaller or the larger?
Adventurers now must emigrate a long way farther.

And sometimes they retell the tales of former times,
When ships went down, and other ships sailed on,
When sickness raged, flood-waters climbed,
When murderers struck – survivors carried on,
When cities fell, and other cities – strong! –
That built upon the graves of those who died
Strange monuments under more distant skies.

Where once there slumbered empty spaces deep,
Stranger to feeling, will and consciousness,
Now there criss-cross fragile vessels of hope,
Breasting the waves of darkness, gales of angry light,
Testing the purpose of a cunning race
Among the asteroids, the outer satellites,
The nuclear mines of the new Prometheus.

I love you, cities of a hundred worlds!
Where swindlers hustle, as they always did,
And in your streets live *killers, angels, refugees,*
And lovers turn their backs in bitterness –
Yet through it all we're glad to be alive,
To strive to taste forbidden happiness,
To join our hands and cry – We shall be blessed!

Across the living brink of crystal deeps
Flies the gathering spirit with sky-challenging gaze.
A breath of love – it cries – an ounce of vision,
A disciple's patience and a master's reason,
A scream of pain emerging from a mother's bosom,
An urge to live and put life to the test,
A longing that simply cannot be suppressed –

These are the heartbeat of a zillion suns,
The sense unseeing in the living atoms
That weaves them into self-sustaining patterns,
The thought unknowing in the cosmic waste
That dreams up you and me to live in haste
And build our little worlds in hope and passion –
    The acolytes of INFINITE CREATION !